# WORK~~BOOK~~

## For

# Calling in "The One"

## 7 Weeks to Attract the Love of Your Life

*(A Guide to Katherine Woodward Thomas's Book)*

Wisdom Reads

*This Companion Workbook is intended to be used as a supplement to the original book. It is not meant to replace the original book, but rather to enhance and deepen the understanding of the concepts presented in the original book*

# Contents

# How To Use This Workbook

This workbook is designed to be used in conjunction with the original book. It provides a summary of the book, as well as key lessons and self-reflection questions for each chapter. The self-reflection questions are designed to help you think about and apply the concepts from the book to your own life.

To use the workbook, simply start by reading the summary of the book. This will give you a general overview of the material. Then, turn to the chapter that you are interested in. Read the key takeaways and answer the self-reflection questions. Take your time and really think about your answers. The self-reflection questions are an important part of the learning process.

In addition to self-reflection, the workbook includes a series of implementation exercises. These exercises are designed to be practical applications of the ideas presented in the book. Each exercise is carefully crafted to guide you through a transformative experience, enabling you to actively apply the concepts to your life. Engaging in these exercises will help you gain firsthand experience and cultivate new habits, attitudes, and perspectives.

At the end of the workbook, there is a section titled Self Evaluation Questions. These questions are designed to help you assess your progress and identify areas where you need to improve. Take some time to answer these questions honestly. This will help you to identify your strengths and weaknesses and to develop a plan for improvement.

We hope that this workbook will be a valuable tool in your personal growth journey. Remember that this workbook is meant to be a supplement to the original book, not a replacement. Use it to your advantage and you will be well on your way to success.

# Summary

"Calling in "The One" Revised and Expanded: 7 Weeks to Attract the Love of Your Life" by Katherine Woodward Thomas is a self-help book that provides a comprehensive guide to finding true love and creating a fulfilling romantic relationship. This revised and expanded edition builds upon the author's original work, offering updated insights and additional exercises to support readers on their journey to attract their ideal partner.

The book begins by acknowledging the importance of self-reflection and inner work in preparing oneself for a loving and committed relationship. Katherine Woodward Thomas emphasizes the significance of self-love, self-worth, and personal growth as essential foundations for attracting a compatible and fulfilling partner. Through various exercises, meditations, and journaling prompts, readers are encouraged to explore their own beliefs, patterns, and emotional baggage that may be blocking them from experiencing the love they desire.

Over the course of seven weeks, the book provides a step-by-step program that takes readers through a transformative process. Each week focuses on a specific theme and includes practical exercises, affirmations, and meditations designed to deepen self-awareness and shift old patterns. The themes covered include clarifying one's vision of love, releasing past hurts and resentments, embracing forgiveness, enhancing self-confidence, and aligning with one's desires.

Katherine Woodward Thomas draws from her own personal experiences and the insights gained from working with countless clients as a relationship coach. She offers practical tools for navigating dating, setting healthy boundaries, and communicating effectively to create a strong foundation for a lasting partnership.

One of the key concepts explored in the book is the idea of calling in "The One" rather than merely seeking a relationship. This approach encourages readers to cultivate a mindset of openness, trust, and belief that their ideal partner is out there and will be drawn to them when the time is right. By focusing on personal growth and self-improvement, readers learn to attract a partner who is aligned with their authentic selves and shared values.

# Week One |Preparing For Love

## Key Takeaways

1. Expanding your capacity to love and be loved involves a process of self-discovery and self-care. It means acknowledging and addressing any past hurts or emotional baggage that may be inhibiting your ability to give and receive love. This can be achieved through various practices such as journaling, therapy, meditation, and engaging in activities that promote self-love and healing.

2. Looking through Laura's eyes refers to adopting a perspective that aligns with the qualities and attributes you admire in the person you desire to attract. By envisioning yourself from their viewpoint, you can identify the positive aspects of yourself that would be appealing to them.

3. Accessing the power to manifest a miracle involves developing a strong belief in your ability to manifest what you desire, including love. It requires setting clear intentions about the kind of love you want and taking proactive steps towards achieving it. Maintaining a positive mindset and taking inspired action are essential components of this process, as they help you align with the energy needed to manifest your desired outcome.

4. Starting with the end in mind entails creating a clear and detailed vision of what a loving relationship looks like to you. This involves considering the qualities and dynamics you desire in a partnership, the level of emotional connection and support, and the activities and experiences you envision sharing with your partner. Having a well-defined vision allows you to set specific goals and take purposeful actions to bring that vision to life.

5. Honouring your need for others means acknowledging that humans are inherently social beings and that we thrive on connection and companionship. It involves being open to receiving love from others and recognizing that you are deserving of it. Additionally, it means being willing to give love to others, fostering a mindset of generosity and empathy. By embracing both the capacity to receive and give love, you create an attractive and magnetic energy that draws love into your life.

6. Cultivating a vision of love fulfilled requires actively imagining and embodying the experience of being in a loving relationship. This involves visualizing the emotions, sensations, and joys that come with being deeply connected to a partner. By regularly engaging in this visualization practice, you send a powerful

message to the universe that you are ready and open to receiving love.

7. Making the space for love involves creating an environment in your life that supports the growth and presence of love. This includes clearing away any emotional baggage or negative patterns that may hinder your ability to engage in healthy relationships. It also means prioritizing love in your life by making time for dating, nurturing existing relationships, and engaging in activities that bring you joy and fulfillment. By intentionally making space for love, you create a fertile ground for love to flourish and thrive.

## Self-Reflection Questions

How can you expand your capacity to love and be loved? Are there any past hurts or emotional wounds that require healing? What self-care practices can you engage in to nurture self-love and open your heart to receiving love?

_____

_____

_____

_____

_____

_____

_____

_____

_____

_____

_____

When you imagine looking through Laura's eyes, what qualities do you admire in the person you want to attract? Reflect on those qualities and consider how you possess similar attributes that would be attractive to them. How can you embody and showcase those qualities?

_____

_____

_____

_____

_____

_____

_____

_____

_____

_____

_____

_____

Do you truly believe in your power to manifest a miracle, including love? Take a moment to reflect on any doubts or limiting beliefs you may have about your ability to attract love into your life. How can you strengthen your belief and align your actions with the intention to manifest the loving relationship you desire?

_____

_____

_____

_____

_____

_____

_____

_____

_____

_____

_____

What does a loving relationship look like to you? Take time to reflect on the specific qualities, dynamics, and experiences you envision in your ideal partnership. How can you align your thoughts, actions, and choices with that vision to create a pathway towards its realization?

_____

_____

_____

_____

_____

_____

_____

_____

_____

_____

_____

_____

How do you honor your need for others? Reflect on your ability to receive love from others and your willingness to give love in return. Are there any barriers or resistance preventing you from fully embracing both the act of giving and receiving love? How can you cultivate a more open and generous mindset towards love?

_____

_____

_____

_____

_____

_____

_____

_____

_____

_____

_____

_____

How can you cultivate a vision of love fulfilled in your life? Take a moment to imagine what it would be like to be in a loving relationship. Reflect on the emotions, experiences, and connections you desire. How can you integrate this vision into your daily thoughts, visualizations, and actions to create a magnetic energy that attracts love?

_____

_____

_____

_____

_____

_____

_____

_____

_____

_____

_____

Are there any emotional baggage or negative patterns that you need to clear to make space for love? Reflect on any unresolved issues or limiting beliefs that might hinder your ability to engage in healthy relationships. How can you release and heal from these patterns?

_____

_____

_____

_____

_____

_____

_____

_____

_____

_____

_____

_____

# Life-Changing Exercises

1. Set aside dedicated time each day to journal about your self-love journey. Reflect on your strengths, accomplishments, and qualities you love about yourself. Write down affirmations and positive self-talk to reinforce your self-worth and foster a deeper sense of self-love.

2. Incorporate regular meditation sessions into your routine specifically focused on healing past hurts and emotional wounds. Use guided meditations or visualization techniques to bring awareness to these areas, release negative emotions, and cultivate forgiveness and self-compassion.

3. Create a visual representation of your ideal loving relationship. Gather images, quotes, and symbols that reflect the qualities and experiences you desire. Display the vision board in a prominent place to remind yourself of your relationship goals and manifest them into reality.

4. Acts of Love and Kindness: Challenge yourself to perform acts of love and kindness towards others on a daily basis. This can include simple gestures such as offering a listening ear, giving compliments, or performing random acts of kindness. By actively

giving love, you cultivate a mindset of abundance and attract positive energy into your life.

5. Design a ritual to symbolically release emotional baggage and negative patterns from your past. This can be done through activities like writing down what you wish to let go of, then burning or tearing up the paper as a symbolic act of releasing those burdens. Follow this ritual with self-care practices and affirmations to reinforce your commitment to a new chapter free from emotional baggage.

6. Dedicate time each day to practice a visualization meditation where you imagine yourself in a loving relationship. Visualize the emotions, connection, and experiences you desire. Engage all your senses to make the visualization vivid and real. This practice helps align your subconscious mind with your conscious intention to attract love.

7. Create a step-by-step action plan to actively make space for love in your life. This can include joining social groups or dating platforms, attending events where you can meet new people, or engaging in hobbies and activities that align with your interests. Commit to following your action plan and track your progress, celebrating each step forward towards inviting love into your life.

# Week 2 | Completing Your Past

## Key Takeaways

1. Allowing Loss: Completing your past begins with acknowledging and allowing yourself to fully experience any losses or heartbreaks from previous relationships. By embracing your emotions and giving yourself permission to grieve, you create space for healing and growth.

2. Asking a More Beautiful Question: Once you have allowed yourself to grieve, you can begin to ask yourself a more beautiful question about your past relationships. This could be a question like, "What did I learn from this relationship?" or "What will I need to do differently in my next relationship?" A more beautiful question will assist you in finding the silver lining in your prior experiences and learning from them.

3. Letting Go of Your Past: To attract the love of your life, it is essential to release attachments to past relationships. This involves forgiving yourself and others, making peace with the past, and allowing yourself to move forward with a clean slate. By doing so, you create space for new love and opportunities to enter your life.

4. Evolving Toxic Ties: Identify and address any toxic or unhealthy patterns in your past relationships. This involves recognizing the role you played in those dynamics and taking responsibility for your actions. By consciously working on personal growth and breaking free from negative patterns, you pave the way for healthier and more fulfilling connections.

5. Renegotiating Old Agreements: Examine any unspoken or implicit agreements you made with yourself based on past experiences. These agreements may limit your beliefs about love, worthiness, or what you deserve. Challenge and renegotiate these agreements, replacing them with empowering beliefs and standards that align with your desire to attract true love.

6. Appreciating Your Sacred Wounds: Recognize that the wounds and challenges you have faced in your past relationships have the potential to become catalysts for personal growth and transformation. Embrace your sacred wounds as valuable sources of wisdom, resilience, and empathy. By honoring and appreciating these wounds, you can harness their power to attract a loving and authentic partnership.

7. Treating Yourself as You Want to Be Treated: Finally, completing your past involves cultivating self-love and self-care. Treat yourself with the same kindness,

respect, and compassion that you desire from a partner. Set healthy boundaries, prioritize your well-being, and engage in practices that nurture your mind, body, and spirit. By demonstrating self-love, you signal to the universe your readiness to attract a partner who will also cherish and uplift you.

## Self-Reflection Questions

Have you allowed yourself to fully acknowledge and process any losses or heartbreaks from your past relationships? How can you create space for healing and growth in relation to these experiences?

_____

_____

_____

_____

_____

_____

_____

_____

_____

_____

_____

_____

What more beautiful question can you ask yourself to shift your perspective and find meaning in your past relationship experiences? How can reframing your perspective help you grow and transform?

_____

_____

_____

_____

_____

_____

_____

_____

_____

_____

_____

Are there any attachments or unresolved emotions from past relationships that you need to let go of in order to move forward? How can you practice forgiveness and make peace with your past?

_____

_____

_____

_____

_____

_____

_____

_____

_____

_____

_____

_____

Reflect on any toxic or unhealthy patterns that have been present in your past relationships. How have you contributed to these dynamics, and how can you consciously work on personal growth to break free from them?

_____

_____

_____

_____

_____

_____

_____

_____

_____

_____

_____

What unspoken or implicit agreements have you made with yourself based on past relationship experiences? Do these agreements limit your beliefs about love, worthiness, or what you deserve? How can you challenge and renegotiate these agreements to align with your desire for a healthy and fulfilling partnership?

_____

_____

_____

_____

_____

_____

_____

_____

_____

_____

_____

_____

How can you appreciate and honor the wounds and challenges you have faced in your past relationships? What lessons, strengths, or insights have you gained from these experiences that can contribute to your personal growth and readiness for a loving partnership?

_____

_____

_____

_____

_____

_____

_____

_____

_____

_____

_____

_____

Reflect on how you treat yourself on a daily basis. Are you showing yourself the same kindness, respect, and compassion that you desire from a partner? How can you prioritize self-love and self-care, set healthy boundaries, and engage in practices that nurture your overall well-being?

_____

_____

_____

_____

_____

_____

_____

_____

_____

_____

_____

# Life-Changing Exercises

1. Reflection and Release: Take time to reflect on your past relationships and identify any lingering feelings or attachments. Write a letter to yourself or a person from your past expressing your emotions and releasing any negative energy associated with that relationship. Burn or shred the letter as a symbolic act of letting go.

2. Empowering Affirmations: Create a list of affirmations that challenge limiting beliefs about love and worthiness. Repeat these affirmations daily, especially when you catch yourself falling into negative thought patterns.

3. Rebuilding Trust: Identify any trust issues that stem from past relationships and work on rebuilding trust within yourself. Start by setting small goals and commitments to yourself and follow through on them. Gradually expand these commitments and celebrate your accomplishments along the way. This process helps you restore faith in your own ability to trust and be trusted.

4. Gratitude for Lessons Learned: Create a gratitude journal dedicated to acknowledging the valuable lessons you have learned from past relationships. Each day, write down at least three lessons you

gained from those experiences. Cultivating gratitude for the wisdom gained helps shift your focus from the pain of the past to the growth and empowerment it provided.

5. Setting Boundaries: Practice setting and maintaining healthy boundaries in your current relationships and interactions. Pay attention to your needs and feelings, and assertively communicate them to others. When necessary, practice saying "no" and prioritize self-care.. By establishing and upholding boundaries, you create a foundation of respect and self-worth in your relationships.

6. Design a self-love ritual that nurtures your mind, body, and spirit. It could involve activities such as meditation, journaling, taking a soothing bath, practicing self-care routines, engaging in hobbies you enjoy, or spending quality time with yourself. Dedicate regular time to these rituals to cultivate a deeper sense of self-love and appreciation.

# Week Three | Transforming Your Love Identity

## Key Takeaways

1. Connecting the Dots: The first step to transforming your love identity is to connect the dots between your past experiences and your current beliefs about love. This may mean journaling about your past relationships, talking to a therapist, or simply spending some time reflecting on your own experiences. Once you have a better understanding of how your past has shaped your current beliefs, you can begin to challenge those beliefs and create new ones.

2. Naming Your False Love Identity Beliefs: Identify the limiting beliefs or false narratives you have internalized about love and relationships. These beliefs may include notions like "I am unworthy of love" or "Love always ends in heartbreak." By acknowledging and naming these beliefs, you can begin to challenge and transform them.

3. Waking Up to Your True Love Identity: Explore and awaken to your authentic love identity—the qualities, values, and desires that align with your true self. This involves reconnecting with your inner wisdom, passions, and purpose. By aligning your love

identity with your authentic self, you open yourself up to attracting a partner who resonates with your true essence.

4. Relating to Yourself and Others in New Ways: Shift your relationship dynamics by developing new ways of relating to yourself and others. This involves cultivating self-compassion, setting healthy boundaries, and practicing open and honest communication. By consciously choosing to relate in healthier ways, you create a solid foundation for attracting and nurturing a loving relationship.

5. Reclaiming Your Disowned Self: Examine the parts of yourself that you have disowned or suppressed due to past experiences or societal conditioning. Reclaim those aspects and integrate them into your identity. Embracing your whole self allows for a more authentic expression of love and connection.

6. Embracing a Growth Mindset: Adopt a growth mindset when it comes to love and relationships. Embrace challenges, view setbacks as opportunities for growth, and believe in your ability to learn and evolve. A growth mindset fosters resilience, openness, and a willingness to learn from past experiences.

7. Engaging in a Release Ceremony: Create a symbolic ritual or ceremony to release any emotional baggage or negative attachments from your past. This can involve writing a letter of forgiveness, burning old mementos, or engaging in a guided meditation for letting go. By intentionally releasing the past, you make space for new love and transformative experiences to enter your life.

## Self-Reflection Questions

How have you allowed yourself to experience and process loss in your past relationships? Are there any unresolved emotions or grief that still need your attention and healing?

_____

_____

_____

_____

_____

_____

_____

_____

_____

_____

_____

What false beliefs about love and relationships have you been holding onto? How have these beliefs shaped your love identity? How can you challenge and transform them to align with your authentic self?

_____

_____

_____

_____

_____

_____

_____

_____

_____

_____

_____

Are you fully awake and aware of your true love identity? What are the qualities, values, and desires that define your authentic self when it comes to love and relationships?

_____

_____

_____

_____

_____

_____

_____

_____

_____

_____

_____

How do you currently relate to yourself and others in the realm of love? Are there any patterns or dynamics that you need to shift or improve? How can you practice self-compassion and establish healthier boundaries?

_____

_____

_____

_____

_____

_____

_____

_____

_____

_____

_____

_____

Have you disowned any parts of yourself in the context of love and relationships? How can you reclaim and integrate those aspects into your identity to foster a more authentic expression of love?

_____

_____

_____

_____

_____

_____

_____

_____

_____

_____

_____

Do you approach love and relationships with a growth mindset? How do you view challenges and setbacks? Are you open to learning and evolving in the pursuit of love?

_____

_____

_____

_____

_____

_____

_____

_____

_____

_____

_____

Have you engaged in a release ceremony or symbolic ritual to let go of the past? Are there any emotional baggage or negative attachments that you still need to release?

_____

_____

_____

_____

_____

_____

_____

_____

_____

_____

_____

# Life-Changing Exercises

1. Self-Reflection Journaling: Set aside dedicated time each day to journal about the key lessons you have learned about yourself and your love identity. Reflect on how these insights have impacted your past relationships and identify areas for growth and transformation.

2. Self-Compassion Practice: Develop a daily self-compassion practice. Whenever you notice self-critical thoughts or judgments arise, consciously replace them with kind and compassionate affirmations. Treat yourself with the same understanding and kindness you would offer a dear friend.

3. Boundary Setting Exercise: Identify areas in your relationships where you need to set healthier boundaries. Practice communicating your needs and desires assertively but lovingly. Remember that setting boundaries is an act of self-respect and an important aspect of attracting a loving and fulfilling partnership.

4. Embrace Growth Opportunities: Challenge yourself to embrace growth opportunities in your personal and romantic life. Seek out new experiences, engage in activities that expand your comfort zone, and be

open to learning from both successes and failures. Embracing growth will help you evolve into the best version of yourself.

5. Gratitude Practice: Cultivate a daily gratitude practice to shift your focus towards positivity and abundance. Each day, write down three things you are grateful for in relation to yourself, your relationships, or your journey of personal growth. Expressing gratitude amplifies the positive energy and enhances your ability to attract love and fulfillment.

# Week Four | Setting Your Course

## Key Takeaways

1. Expanding Your Vision of What's Possible: In order to attract the love of your life, it is essential to expand your vision of what love can be. Let go of any limitations or preconceived notions you may have about relationships and open yourself up to the infinite possibilities. By broadening your perspective, you create space for the extraordinary to enter your life.

2. Acting on Your Intention: Setting your course requires more than just having the intention to find love; it requires taking action. Be proactive in your pursuit of love by engaging in activities and practices that align with your desire to attract a partner. This could involve joining social groups, trying new hobbies, or attending events where you have the opportunity to meet like-minded individuals.

3. Clarifying Your Soul's Purpose: Take time to reflect on and clarify your soul's purpose. Understanding your own passions, values, and the contribution you want to make to the world will not only bring fulfillment to your own life but also attract a partner who aligns with your purpose. When you are living in alignment

with your soul's purpose, you radiate authenticity and attract those who resonate with your journey.

4. Receiving Inner Guidance: Cultivate a connection with your inner wisdom and intuition. Through practices such as meditation, journaling, or simply taking moments of stillness, you can tap into your inner guidance system. This inner voice will guide you towards choices and actions that are in alignment with your highest good and help you navigate your path to love.

5. Establishing Personal Integrity: Personal integrity is crucial when setting your course to attract the love of your life. It involves aligning your thoughts, words, and actions with your values and highest self. By practicing honesty, authenticity, and staying true to your commitments, you create a solid foundation of trust within yourself and attract partners who value these qualities.

6. Practicing Prayer and Meditation: Prayer and meditation are powerful practices that can support you in setting your course. They help you cultivate a deeper connection with your spirituality, quiet your mind, and create a space for clarity and guidance to emerge. Regularly engaging in these practices can enhance your ability to attract love and maintain a

centered and grounded presence throughout your journey.

7. Making Wise Choices: When setting your course, it is essential to make conscious and wise choices that align with your vision of attracting the love of your life. This involves making choices that honor your values, prioritize your well-being, and support your personal growth. By making intentional decisions in all areas of your life, you create an energetic resonance that attracts a partner who shares your values and is aligned with your path.

## Self-Reflection Questions

What limitations or preconceived notions do you have about relationships, and how can you expand your vision of what love can be for you?

_____

_____

_____

_____

_____

_____

_____

_____

_____

_____

_____

In what ways are you actively taking action to pursue the love of your life? How can you further act on your intention to attract a partner?

_____

_____

_____

_____

_____

_____

_____

_____

_____

_____

_____

What is your soul's purpose, and how does it align with your desire for love? How can you clarify and live in alignment with your purpose to attract a partner who resonates with your journey?

_____

_____

_____

_____

_____

_____

_____

_____

_____

_____

How connected are you to your inner guidance and intuition? What practices can you implement to deepen your connection and trust in your inner wisdom as you navigate your path to love?

_____

_____

_____

_____

_____

_____

_____

_____

_____

_____

_____

_____

Are you consistently practicing personal integrity in your thoughts, words, and actions? How can you ensure that you align your values and maintain trust within yourself as you attract a loving partnership?

_____

_____

_____

_____

_____

_____

_____

_____

_____

_____

_____

_____

How often do you engage in prayer and meditation to support your journey to love? What steps can you take to incorporate these practices more regularly into your life and enhance your spiritual connection?

_____

_____

_____

_____

_____

_____

_____

_____

_____

_____

_____

Are the choices you make in your life aligned with your vision of attracting the love of your life? How can you make wiser and more intentional choices that honor your values, well-being, and personal growth as you create a path towards love?

_____

_____

_____

_____

_____

_____

_____

_____

_____

_____

_____

## Life-Changing Exercises

1. Reflect on Your Vision: Take time to visualize and write down your expanded vision of love and relationships. Be specific about the qualities and characteristics you desire in a partner and the kind of relationship you want to create. Revisit this vision regularly to stay focused and aligned with your intention.

2. Take Inspired Action: Identify one action you can take today that aligns with your intention of attracting love. It could be joining a dating app, signing up for a relationship workshop, or reaching out to a friend to set up a social gathering. By taking proactive steps, you demonstrate your commitment to your desire and open yourself to new possibilities.

3. Explore Your Soul's Purpose: Engage in self-reflection and journaling to gain clarity on your soul's purpose. Ask yourself questions like "What brings me joy?" and "How can I make a difference in the world?" Use this exploration to guide your decisions and actions, allowing your purpose to shine through in all areas of your life, including your journey to finding love.

4. Cultivate Inner Listening: Dedicate regular time for meditation or quiet reflection to cultivate a stronger connection with your inner wisdom. Practice deep

listening to the whispers of your intuition and guidance that arise within you. Trust the messages you receive and follow the insights that resonate with your heart, as they can guide you towards the right choices and opportunities.

5. Embody Personal Integrity: Make a commitment to align your thoughts, words, and actions with your values and highest self. Practice honesty, authenticity, and kindness in your interactions with yourself and others. When you act with integrity, you attract partners who also value these qualities and foster a deeper sense of trust and connection in your relationships.

6. Establish Rituals of Prayer and Meditation: Create a daily practice of prayer and meditation to nurture your spiritual connection and inner peace. Set aside a specific time and space each day to engage in these practices. Allow yourself to be present, surrender any worries or doubts, and cultivate a sense of gratitude for the love that is already present in your life. Trust that your prayers are heard and that you are being guided towards the love you seek.

7. Make Conscious Choices: Evaluate your choices and actions in various areas of your life and ensure they align with your vision of love and your highest good. Consider your daily routines, relationships, and

commitments. Choose activities and engagements that support your well-being and personal growth. By consciously selecting what aligns with your vision, you create an energetic shift that attracts the love and experiences you desire.

# Week Five | First Things First

## Key Takeaways

1. Making commitments: Making a commitment to yourself and your desire to find love is crucial. This involves dedicating time, energy, and resources to your personal growth and relationship goals. By setting clear intentions and making commitments to follow through, you lay the groundwork for a purposeful and focused journey.

2. Developing emotional literacy: Emotional literacy refers to the ability to recognize, understand, and effectively communicate emotions. This point emphasizes the importance of becoming aware of and expressing your emotions in a healthy and constructive manner. By developing emotional literacy, you enhance your self-awareness and deepen your emotional connection with others.

3. Shifting where you're centered: Often, people place their focus and energy outside of themselves, seeking validation and fulfillment from external sources. Shifting where you're centered involves redirecting your focus inward, towards self-love, self-acceptance, and self-worth. This shift allows you to build a solid foundation of self-confidence and self-reliance,

enabling you to attract a loving partner who complements rather than completes you.

4. Giving to yourself what was missing: Many individuals have experienced emotional gaps or deficiencies in their past that may have hindered their ability to attract love. This point highlights the importance of identifying these missing elements and actively giving them to yourself. By nurturing and fulfilling your own emotional needs, you create a sense of wholeness and become more capable of engaging in a healthy, reciprocal relationship.

5. Preparing your body for love: This point emphasizes the connection between physical and emotional well-being. Preparing your body for love involves adopting a lifestyle that supports your overall health and vitality. Engaging in regular exercise, nourishing your body with nutritious foods, and practicing self-care contribute to your physical well-being, enhancing your attractiveness and overall energy to attract a loving partner.

6. Healing your sexuality: A healthy and positive relationship with your own sexuality is essential when calling in "The One." This point encourages exploring and healing any past wounds or limiting beliefs surrounding your sexuality. By embracing your authentic sexual expression, releasing shame or guilt,

and cultivating a sense of empowerment, you can create a safe and fulfilling space for intimacy within a future relationship.

7. Cultivating solitude: Solitude, in this context, refers to intentionally creating space and time for yourself, free from external distractions. This point emphasizes the importance of self-reflection, introspection, and personal growth. Cultivating solitude allows you to deepen your connection with your inner self, understand your desires and values more clearly, and create a strong sense of self-awareness and self-love as you journey towards attracting the love of your life.

## Self-Reflection Questions

What commitments are you willing to make to yourself in order to attract the love of your life? How can you prioritize and dedicate time, energy, and resources towards your personal growth and relationship goals?

_____

_____

_____

_____

_____

_____

_____

_____

_____

_____

_____

_____

How well-developed is your emotional literacy? Are you able to recognize, understand, and effectively communicate your emotions? How can you further enhance your emotional intelligence to deepen your self-awareness and emotional connection with others?

_____

_____

_____

_____

_____

_____

_____

_____

_____

_____

_____

Where are you currently centered in your life? Are you seeking validation and fulfillment externally or do you focus on self-love, self-acceptance, and self-worth? How can you shift your center towards a place of self-confidence and self-reliance?

_____

_____

_____

_____

_____

_____

_____

_____

_____

_____

_____

_____

What emotional needs were missing or unfulfilled in your past? How can you actively give to yourself what was missing? How can you nurture and fulfill your own emotional needs, creating a sense of wholeness and readiness for a healthy, reciprocal relationship?

_____

_____

_____

_____

_____

_____

_____

_____

_____

_____

_____

How well are you preparing your body for love? Are you engaging in regular exercise, nourishing your body with nutritious foods, and practicing self-care? What steps can you take to improve your physical well-being, enhance your attractiveness, and boost your overall energy to attract a loving partner?

_____

_____

_____

_____

_____

_____

_____

_____

_____

_____

_____

_____

Have you explored and healed any past wounds or limiting beliefs surrounding your sexuality? How do you feel about your authentic sexual expression? Are there any remaining shame or guilt that you need to release? What steps can you take to create a safe and empowering space for intimacy within a future relationship?

_____

_____

_____

_____

_____

_____

_____

_____

_____

_____

_____

How often do you cultivate solitude and create space for self-reflection? Do you make time to connect with your inner self, understand your desires and values, and foster self-awareness and self-love? How can you prioritize and integrate moments of solitude into your life to support your personal growth and journey towards attracting the love of your life?

_____

_____

_____

_____

_____

_____

_____

_____

_____

_____

_____

# Life-Changing Exercises

1. Making commitments: Write down a list of all the things you're committed to, both big and small. This could include your goals, your relationships, your health, and your career. Once you have your list, take some time to reflect on each item and how committed you really are. Are there any areas where you could be more committed?

2. Developing emotional literacy: Take some time each day to journal about your emotions. What are you feeling? Why are you feeling that way? How can you express your emotions in a healthy way? The more you understand your emotions, the better equipped you'll be to deal with them in a healthy way.

3. Shifting where you're centered: Spend some time each day meditating or doing another form of mindfulness practice. This will help you to focus on the present moment and to quiet your mind. When you're centered, you're more likely to attract positive experiences into your life.

4. Giving to yourself what was missing: Think about what you needed as a child but didn't receive. Was it love, support, attention, or something else? Once you know what you needed, start to give it to yourself. This could involve doing things that make

you happy, spending time with loved ones, or simply taking some time for yourself each day.

5. Preparing your body for love: Eat healthy foods, exercise regularly, and get enough sleep. When you take care of your body, you're sending a signal to the universe that you're ready for love.

6. Healing your sexuality: If you have any negative beliefs or experiences around sex, it's important to heal them. Create a safe and sacred space to explore and heal your sexuality. Engage in practices such as guided meditations, therapy, or workshops that specifically address sexual healing. Release any shame or guilt associated with your sexuality and embrace your authentic expression. Journal about your experiences and celebrate the progress you make in this journey of sexual healing.

7. Cultivating solitude: Spend some time each day alone. This could involve going for a walk in nature, reading a book, or simply sitting in silence. When you're able to be comfortable with yourself, you're more likely to attract a healthy and loving relationship.

# Week Six | A Life Worth Living

## Key Takeaways

1. Being Generous: Embracing a spirit of generosity enhances our relationships and attracts love into our lives. By giving our time, attention, and support to others, we demonstrate kindness and empathy. Generosity extends beyond material possessions; it encompasses compassion, understanding, and a willingness to lend a helping hand.

2. Choosing to be Happy: Happiness is an inside job. By consciously choosing happiness, we cultivate a positive mindset that radiates joy and attracts others. When we focus on self-care, pursue our passions, and find contentment within ourselves, we become a magnet for love. Our happiness becomes infectious, drawing potential partners who are drawn to our positive energy.

3. Owning Yourself as Cause: Taking responsibility for our actions, choices, and emotions empowers us to create the life we desire. By embracing the belief that we have control over our own destiny, we shift from a victim mentality to one of empowerment. When we own ourselves as cause, we become the architects of our love life, making intentional decisions that align with our values and desires.

4.  Living the Questions: Rather than seeking definitive answers, living the questions encourages us to explore and grow. It involves being open to the unknown and embracing the process of self-discovery. By approaching life with curiosity and an open mind, we invite opportunities for personal growth and deeper connections with others.

5.  Listening with an Open Heart: Effective communication is vital in attracting and maintaining a healthy relationship. Listening with an open heart involves actively hearing and understanding others without judgment or preconceived notions. By practicing deep listening, we create a safe and supportive space for our partner's thoughts and feelings, fostering a strong bond built on trust and mutual understanding.

6.  Speaking Up: Expressing our needs, desires, and boundaries is crucial for establishing healthy relationships. By speaking up, we honor ourselves and ensure that our needs are met. Honest and open communication strengthens connections and allows for genuine intimacy. When we courageously share our authentic selves, we attract partners who appreciate and respect our voice.

7.  Becoming "The One": Becoming "The One" refers to becoming the best version of ourselves in

preparation for attracting a loving partner. This entails self-reflection, personal growth, and continuously striving to be the person we want to be in a relationship. By investing in self-improvement, we cultivate self-love and become a magnet for a partner who values and complements our growth journey.

## Self-Reflection Questions

How can you practice being more generous in your daily interactions with others? What actions can you take to show kindness, empathy, and support to those around you?

---

---

---

---

---

---

---

---

---

---

Are you actively choosing happiness in your life? What self-care practices or activities bring you joy and contentment? How can you prioritize these activities to enhance your overall happiness?

_____

_____

_____

_____

_____

_____

_____

_____

_____

_____

_____

_____

In what areas of your life can you take more ownership and responsibility? How can you shift from a victim mentality to one of empowerment and become the cause of positive change in your life?

_____

_____

_____

_____

_____

_____

_____

_____

_____

_____

_____

How can you embrace the unknown and allow yourself to explore and grow? What steps can you take to foster curiosity and open-mindedness in your journey of self-discovery?

_____

_____

_____

_____

_____

_____

_____

_____

_____

_____

_____

How well do you listen with an open heart to others? Do you actively practice deep listening without judgment or preconceived notions? What can you do to create a safe and supportive space for others to express themselves?

_____

_____

_____

_____

_____

_____

_____

_____

_____

_____

_____

Are you speaking up and expressing your needs, desires, and boundaries in your relationships? How can you communicate more honestly and openly to foster genuine intimacy and ensure your needs are met? What steps can you take to honor your voice?

_____

_____

_____

_____

_____

_____

_____

_____

_____

_____

_____

Reflect on your journey of becoming "The One." What areas of personal growth are you currently focusing on? How can you continue investing in self-improvement to cultivate self-love and attract a partner who aligns with your values and growth journey?

_____

_____

_____

_____

_____

_____

_____

_____

_____

_____

_____

# Life-Changing Exercises

1. Random Acts of Kindness: Practice being generous by committing to perform one random act of kindness every day. It could be as simple as offering a sincere compliment, helping someone in need, or volunteering for a cause you care about. Observe how these acts of generosity not only impact others but also bring a sense of fulfillment and joy to your own life.

2. Choosing to be happy: Start each day by making a conscious decision to be happy. Take some time to think about all the things you are grateful for, and focus on the positive aspects of your life.

3. Personal Responsibility Audit: Conduct a personal responsibility audit by reflecting on your actions, choices, and emotions. Take ownership of any areas where you have been blaming others or playing the victim. Identify one area where you can take proactive steps to assume responsibility and make positive changes. Implement those changes and observe the impact it has on your relationships and overall well-being.

4. Reflective Journaling: Engage in reflective journaling by living the questions. Set aside dedicated time each week to write about the deeper questions of life,

love, and personal growth. Explore your thoughts, beliefs, and desires openly on paper. Allow yourself to embrace the process of self-discovery and gain clarity on what truly matters to you.

5. Active Listening Practice: Develop your active listening skills by consciously practicing listening with an open heart. Engage in a conversation with a friend or loved one and focus on genuinely hearing and understanding their perspective without interrupting or formulating responses in your mind. Take note of how this deep listening strengthens your connection with others and allows for more meaningful conversations.

6. Speaking up: When you have something to say, don't be afraid to say it. Don't be afraid to share your ideas, your opinions, and your feelings. The world needs to hear your voice. Notice the positive impact this has on your relationships as you establish healthy communication patterns and gain a sense of empowerment.

7. Personal Growth Plan: Create a personal growth plan to become "The One" you aspire to be. Set specific goals and action steps to enhance different aspects of your life, such as emotional well-being, physical health, career development, and personal interests. Evaluate your progress on a regular basis and make

improvements as appropriate. Embrace the journey of self-improvement and observe how it positively influences your self-love and attracts aligned partners.

# Week Seven | Living Love Fulfilled

## Key Takeaways

1. Living an enchanted life: An enchanted life is one that is filled with wonder, joy, and magic. It is a life that is lived with passion and purpose. When you live an enchanted life, you are open to the possibilities of the world and you are willing to take risks. You are not afraid to step outside of your comfort zone and you are always looking for new ways to grow and learn.

2. Generating love: Love is not just something we seek from others; it is a powerful force that we can actively generate within ourselves. By practicing self-love, self-care, and acts of kindness, we create an abundant reservoir of love that not only nourishes us but also attracts love from others.

3. Expanding from "Me" to "We": Finding love involves transitioning from a self-centered perspective to one that embraces connection and partnership. This shift entails recognizing that a fulfilling relationship requires a balance between individual needs and the needs of a partnership, fostering mutual growth, and creating a strong foundation for love to flourish.

4. Forgiving Yourself and Others: Forgiveness is a transformative act that liberates us from the burden

of past hurts and resentments. By forgiving ourselves and others, we release negative energy and make space for love to enter our lives. This practice opens our hearts and allows us to approach relationships with compassion, understanding, and a willingness to heal.

5. Being grateful for it all: Gratitude is a powerful practice that helps us shift our focus from lack to abundance. By cultivating gratitude for the blessings in our lives, even during challenging times, we align ourselves with the positive energy of love. Expressing gratitude attracts more love and blessings, creating a virtuous cycle of abundance and fulfillment.

6. Becoming unstoppable: To attract the love we desire, we must cultivate an unwavering belief in ourselves and our ability to create the life we envision. Becoming unstoppable means developing resilience, determination, and a growth mindset. By embracing challenges as opportunities for growth, we become empowered to overcome obstacles on our path to love.

7. Holding the high watch: Holding the high watch refers to maintaining a positive and optimistic perspective, even in the face of setbacks or disappointments. It involves trusting that the love we seek is on its way and remaining open to unexpected

possibilities. By holding the high watch, we emit a powerful signal to the universe that we are ready and deserving of love, attracting it towards us.

## Self-Reflection Questions

How can you cultivate a sense of enchantment and wonder in your daily life to attract more love and joy?

_____

_____

_____

_____

_____

_____

_____

_____

_____

_____

In what ways are you actively generating love within yourself and spreading it to others? How can you further nurture and expand this love within you?

_____

_____

_____

_____

_____

_____

_____

_____

_____

_____

_____

Are you open to transitioning from a "Me" mindset to a "We" mindset in your relationships? How can you strike a healthy balance between your individual needs and the needs of a partnership?

_____

_____

_____

_____

_____

_____

_____

_____

_____

_____

_____

Have you forgiven yourself for past mistakes and shown compassion towards others who may have hurt you? How can you deepen your practice of forgiveness to create space for more love in your life?

_____

_____

_____

_____

_____

_____

_____

_____

_____

_____

_____

_____

How often do you express gratitude for the blessings in your life, even during challenging times? Are there any areas where you can cultivate a greater sense of gratitude to attract more love and abundance?

_____

_____

_____

_____

_____

_____

_____

_____

_____

_____

_____

Are you embracing challenges as opportunities for growth and believing in your ability to create the love you desire? How can you develop a mindset of resilience and determination to overcome obstacles on your path to love?

_____

_____

_____

_____

_____

_____

_____

_____

_____

_____

_____

Are you holding the high watch by maintaining a positive and optimistic perspective, regardless of setbacks or disappointments? How can you strengthen your trust in the universe and remain open to unexpected possibilities in your journey towards love?

_____

_____

_____

_____

_____

_____

_____

_____

_____

_____

_____

## Life-Changing Exercises

1. Each day, find a few moments to immerse yourself in the enchantment of life. It could be watching a beautiful sunset, savoring a delicious meal, or listening to your favorite music. Take note of these moments and journal about the joy and wonder they bring, allowing yourself to fully experience the magic in everyday life.

2. Set aside dedicated time each week to generate love within yourself. Engage in activities that make you feel loved and cared for, such as taking a relaxing bath, practicing self-affirmations, or indulging in a hobby you enjoy. Actively cultivate a loving mindset and observe how it impacts your overall well-being and attracts love into your life.

3. We-Centered Actions: Identify one area in your life where you can shift from a "me" mindset to a "we" mindset. It could be involving your partner or loved ones in decision-making, actively seeking opportunities to support and uplift others, or finding ways to contribute to your community. Reflect on how these actions foster connection and create a more harmonious and fulfilling environment.

4. Forgiveness Practice: Choose one person, including yourself, whom you want to forgive. Write a heartfelt

forgiveness letter expressing your willingness to let go of resentment and embrace healing. You can choose to send the letter or keep it for your personal growth. Reflect on the emotional release and freedom forgiveness brings, and notice how it impacts your ability to attract and receive love.

5. Start a daily gratitude practice by writing down three things you are grateful for each day. Be specific and genuine in acknowledging even the smallest blessings. Over time, you will cultivate a mindset of abundance and appreciation, shifting your focus towards the positive aspects of life. Observe how gratitude enhances your overall well-being and attracts more love and abundance into your experience.

6. Take on a challenge that pushes you out of your comfort zone. It could be learning a new skill, pursuing a passion project, or facing a fear. Throughout the process, embrace a mindset of resilience, determination, and growth. Notice the personal growth and self-confidence that emerges as you overcome obstacles, and let this newfound strength radiate into your love life.

7. Start a journal where you record your experiences of holding the high watch. Whenever you encounter setbacks or disappointments in your love life, write

about how you maintain a positive and optimistic perspective. Explore the lessons and growth opportunities within these experiences, and note the positive shifts that occur as you stay open to love's possibilities.

# Self-Assessment Questions

Have you actively engaged with the content in the workbook and completed all the exercises?

_____

_____

_____

_____

_____

_____

_____

_____

_____

_____

Were you able to understand and apply the concepts discussed in the workbook to your own life?

_____

_____

_____

_____

_____

_____

_____

_____

_____

_____

_____

Were you able to identify your strengths and weaknesses based on the activities in the workbook?

_____

_____

_____

_____

_____

_____

_____

_____

_____

_____

_____

Did you set clear goals for yourself at the beginning of the workbook, and did you make progress towards achieving them?

_____

_____

_____

_____

_____

_____

_____

_____

_____

_____

_____

_____

How effectively did you apply the strategies and techniques provided in the workbook to overcome challenges or obstacles?

_____

_____

_____

_____

_____

_____

_____

_____

_____

_____

_____

Did you maintain consistency and follow through with the workbook's exercises and activities?

_____

_____

_____

_____

_____

_____

_____

_____

_____

_____

How satisfied are you with your overall progress and development as a result of working through the workbook?

_____

_____

_____

_____

_____

_____

_____

_____

_____

_____

_____

Made in the USA
Middletown, DE
24 April 2024